Adobe Photoshop Elements 3.0 Idea Kit

Adobe Press,
Berkeley, California

Adobe Photoshop Elements 3.0 Idea Kit

Lisa Matthews

Copyright © 2005 by Lisa Matthews

This Adobe Press book was published by Peachpit Press.

Peachpit Press
1249 Eighth Street
Berkeley, CA 94710
510/524-2178
510/524-2221 (fax)
www.peachpit.com

To report errors, please send a note to errata@peachpit.com

Peachpit Press is a division of Pearson Education.

For the latest on Adobe Press books, go to www.adobepress.com/

Editor: Suzie Lowey
Production Editor: Becky Winter
Copyeditor: Liz Welch
Indexer: FireCrystal Communications
CD Production: Eric Geoffroy
Cover Production: Mimi Heft
Cover Illustration: Lisa Matthews

ISBN 0-321-27079-7

9 8 7 6 5 4 3 2 1

Printed and bound in the United States of America

Contents

Introduction

The *Adobe Photoshop Elements 3.0 Idea Kit* delivers ideas, techniques, and templates to help you create exciting and professional-looking digital artwork using Photoshop® Elements 3.0.

Working with your own images, logos, and artwork, you will learn how to use Photoshop Elements to the fullest.

The accompanying CD-ROM offers templates, textures, and borders. Use them with your own imagery to create printed pieces, slide presentations, and Web pages.

The projects range from touching up photographs to creating newsletters, slides, postcards, posters, CD covers, ads, and Web page graphics.

To get your images ready for any of the projects you use, follow the instructions in the Quick Fixes section: From there go to the project of your choice. All the projects contain stand-alone instructions, so just find the project suited to your needs, and get going!

Using the templates

The templates on the CD use only basic fonts available on any computers. You can choose other fonts to customize your artwork. For more font choices, visit the Adobe Web site at www.adobe.com. Adobe's Web site also has information on other Adobe software you may be interested in.

Using the projects

Each project has step-by-step instructions and design tips. Many projects also include design variations and a choice of templates to help you customize your work.

New Features

Photoshop Elements 3.0 has some huge new features that will help you organize and find your files.

Using File Browser

(Mac and PC) In Editor the File Browser lets you browse through your files viewing only the image files. Here you can easily find, move, and rename photo files around your hard drive. The photos appear in a preview box as well as in a multi-image thumbnail view. Metadata and all the technical information about the image is displayed in the box below the preview pane.

Note: Images are only displayed, not stored, in Photoshop Elements 3.0. They are stored in their original folder location.

WINDOWS only Note: Projects 16 and 17 are about using the Organizer. If you are on a Windows machine, you may want to go through these projects first to understand how it works.

Using Organizer and Creations

Photoshop Elements 3.0 has a powerful Organizer that locates all of your images from folders throughout your system and displays them in a Photo Browser. Now you can see all your images from your separate photo files, email attachments, and deeply nested folders in one place. Photo Browser allows you to scroll through photos and adjust their size from small thumbnails to full size. The Timeline bar above lets you quickly locate photos from a specific month and year.

Tags and Collections, while appearing as simple organization tools, are actually a powerful database. Collections lets you pull together files from anywhere on your computer to create groupings like a photo album. Tags lets you mark photos and put them into categories and subcategories. Creations is a one-stop place that automates creating cards, scrapbooks, galleries, and PDFs.

Quick Fixes: Get Your Photos Ready for Projects

Learn easy ways to fix problems such as red-eye, color imbalance, crooked images, and more.

In this first project, you will learn to use some of Photoshop Elements' features to fix common image problems such as red-eye, color casts, and backlighting. Open an image that you'd like to work on. Use the techniques that are best suited to your image.

Before you start to edit your image, take a look at the following checklist to help ensure a smooth project workflow.

Create a copy of the original image. It's always a good idea to keep the original version of your photo as a backup in case you need it for any reason.

Work in RGB Mode. In Photoshop Elements, you can work in RGB, Bitmap, Grayscale, or Index color mode. Very rarely will you work in any other mode than RGB. To see what mode your image is in or to change the mode, choose Image > Mode.

Use the correct image size

Since most projects you will work on, in this book or otherwise, call for a specific dimension, it is important to know how to set the image size.

Whether you are scanning the image yourself, using a digital camera, or simply getting your images from a

photo CD, you should know a little about image resolution.

Images in Photoshop Elements are made of pixels. Pixels are small data squares with a specific color value and location.

The resolution of the image refers to the number of pixels per inch (ppi). The rule of thumb is that higher resolution equals higher image quality simply because there is more information. A higher resolution also means a larger file size.

What does this mean for you? First, to check the resolution of your image, choose Image > Resize > Image Size.

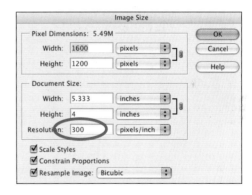

Notice that the dialog box that appears has two different sections. One gives you the actual pixel dimensions—the size the image will appear on screen—and the other gives you the document size—the resolution and print dimensions plus the file size.

Set the resolution

You can change the resolution and print dimensions of the image by entering a higher or lower value. When you do this and the Resample Image box is checked, Photoshop Elements will either add pixels (sample up) or throw them away (downsample). Another rule of thumb: Never sample your images up. Doing so will result in poor image quality as Photoshop Elements can only estimate what information to add; however, downsampling to make your image smaller is generally fine. Ideally, use an image with the resolution and size closest to what is needed for the final output. To get an idea of what resolutions to use, look at the following examples.

16K file size
72 x 108 pixel dim.
1"x 1.5" print size
72 ppi resolution

176K file size
200 x 300 pixel dim.
1" x 1.5" print size
200 ppi resolution

72 ppi—For screen viewing of Web pages or online materials.

120 to 150 ppi—For output to typical desktop laser and ink-jet printers.

A 72 ppi image (left) resampled up to 150 ppi (right) results in poor image quality.

A 300 ppi image (left) downsampled to 150 ppi (right) results in adequate image quality.

200 to 250 ppi—For most professional offset presses used for color magazines and brochures.

Crop and straighten your photo

Look at your image. Is it straight? Do you want to use the whole image or just a section? There are several ways to crop and straighten your image. The one you choose will depend on how much you want to crop.

Trim and straighten your photo.
If your image is crooked because of a sloppy scan, the easiest way to fix it is to choose Image > Rotate > Straighten and Crop Image. Elements will automatically crop and straighten it for you.

Perhaps your image is crooked because of a bad camera angle, or maybe you just want to get rid of an insignificant element in the outer corner. Select the Crop tool (🔲) from the toolbox. Then click and drag around the area of the image that you want to keep. Once the area is selected, you can perform any of the following actions:

- Drag a corner or edge to resize the area of the crop.

- Place the cursor over a corner handle and drag in the direction you want to rotate.

- Place the cursor inside the bounding box and drag to reposition it.

When trying to straighten your image, find a true 90-degree angle to use to align your cropping tool. Pillars and picture frames work well, for example.

When you have finished, press Enter to complete the crop. If you change your mind, press Esc to cancel.

Variation: Crop to an exact dimension and resolution

You may occasionally need to crop to an exact dimension and resolution. For example, you may need a head shot that is 1 inch by 1 inch and 150 dpi. To achieve this, select the Crop tool. Notice that the options bar now gives you a place to enter height, width, and resolution. Enter your values. Now when you drag the cropping tool, it will allow only those dimensions.

Make sure that the image resolution is higher than or equal to the one to which you are cropping to avoid sampling up.

Red Eye Removal tool

The common problem of red-eye is now easily fixed using the Red Eye Removal tool ( ). In either Quick Fix or Standard Editor you can quickly and easily change eyes back to their correct color.

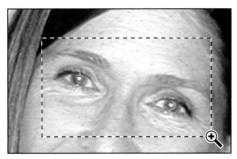

Zoom in. It's always a good idea to zoom in on the area you want to edit so you can see the details. Choose the Zoom tool ( ) from the toolbox. Click on the area of the red eyes until it's big enough to work with.

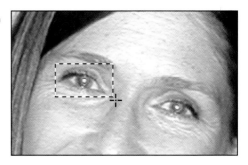

Remove the red. Select the Red Eye Removal tool ( ) and then click and drag the crosshair cursor around the red eye. The red eye will be fixed once you release the mouse. Repeat for the second eye and you've finished!

Healing Brush tool

 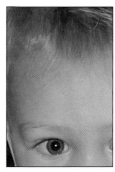

The Healing Brush allows you to get rid of minor dermal imperfections from your photo subjects by sampling a good area and then applying that sample to the bad area. The Healing Brush feature ( ) is split into two parts, the Spot Healing Brush tool (commonly referred to as the "zit zapper") and the Healing Brush tool. The former is for small spots and the latter for larger areas.

1. **Select your brush.** To use either function click and hold on the arrow in the corner of the Healing Brush icon in the toolbar and choose the desired option. Above, in the options bar choose the size and type of brush you need.

2. **Spot be gone!** Alt/Option-click on an area that you want to sample. Then click on the area you want to cover up. Poof! The spot is gone!

Correct the lighting

Correct for backlighting. Often you may take a picture where the foreground is dark and the background is perfectly exposed. The subject could be in front of a window, a sunset, or some other light source. The ideal way to avoid this problem is use an on-camera flash. Even so, some of your photos will have backlighting problems. Fortunately, Photoshop Elements provides a feature that easily remedies the problem.

To correct lighting problems, choose Enhance > Adjust Lighting > Shadows/Highlights. Make sure that the Preview box is checked; then use the sliders to adjust the shadows, highlights, and contrast until you are satisfied with the results.

Enhance your colors

Sometimes your photo may have an unnatural color tint. Fluorescent lighting, tungsten lights, and bad scans are just a few of the potential culprits. There are a couple of good ways to fix this in Photoshop Elements 3.0.

Correct color casts. To remove a distinct color cast select Enhance > Adjust Color > Remove Color Cast. Move your cursor into the image area and click on an area that is supposed to be either gray, white, or black. This will probably do the trick. If it doesn't, another way to correct your color is in the Quick Fix mode.

First, find the Color palette in the menu bin and click the Auto button. Then, use the sliders for Saturation, Hue, Temperature and Tint for any fine-tuning.

Sharpen the photo

Many photos can use a little sharpening. The Unsharp Mask filter works great to sharpen image details. If you have adjusted the resolution of your image, it is best to make this the final step of your photo correction.

1 **Set the zoom percentage to 100%.** Double-click the Zoom tool (🔍) to set the photo to 100% magnification.

2 **Sharpen the image.** Choose Filter > Sharpen > Unsharp Mask. Select the Amount slider and drag until you see a positive result. To preview a specific part of the image, place the cursor in the regular image and move it to the specific area of interest (the cursor will turn into a box). You might want to look closely at hair, eyes, and foliage, where sharpening can be dramatic. It's easy to apply this tool to fix blurry pictures, but over sharpening can also leave your image with a distracting grainy texture.

Save the file

If you are happy with the final results of your image, choose File > Save As, rename the file, and save it in Photoshop format (.psd).

Project 1

Make Your Subject Stand Out

Put your subject in a whole new setting by manipulating the background or changing it altogether.

A fun and easy way to make sure that your subject is the focal point of your photo is to use Photoshop Elements' Selection Brush tool (). This tool allows you to select and separate your subject from the background so you can edit it or change it completely.

1 **Get started.** Open the image you want to edit in Photoshop Elements.

2 **Zoom in on your subject.** Using the Zoom tool (🔍), click an edge of the foreground subject.

3 **Set masking options.** With the Selection Brush tool you create your selections by painting the area you want to select either in Selection mode or Mask mode. In Mask mode, the Selection Brush tool selects the inverse of what you are selecting while giving you a colored preview of the mask you are creating over your subject.

Once you have zoomed in on your subject, select the Selection Brush tool (). On the options bar, select the Mask mode. Set the opacity to 50%. You can also change the mask color or leave it set to the default red.

This will allow you to see the selection mask you are creating over your subject more clearly.

4 **Choose your brush.** Now that you have set your mask options, you want to do the same for your brush.

Click the Brushes pop-up menu. As you can see by scrolling through the list, there are many options. Start with a medium-size soft brush.

5

Select your edges. To make your life easier, first set the edge boundaries and then move inward. Start by painting around the edges of your subject. We are using a soft brush to avoid the harsh cutout look. A softer selection around your subject allows you to blend your final background in a more natural fashion. If you accidentally paint where you don't want to, switch to Selection mode on the options bar and paint over the area.

Photoshop Elements' Selection Brush Mask mode allows you to easily select odd-shaped areas in your image. If you are in Mask mode, a temporary colored overlay appears over the unselected areas and exposes the selected areas of the image. When you toggle back to Selection mode, you will see the "marching ants" marquee around the selection you made.

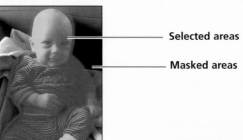

———— Selected areas

———— Masked areas

Painting with the Selection Brush in Mask mode gives you a colored preview of the area you are masking out.

When you toggle back to Selection mode, you will see the resulting selection.

Complete the mask. Once you've finished selecting the edge of your subject, select a larger, hard-edged brush from the Brushes menu. Paint freely inside your new edge until your subject is covered.

Select your subject. Toggle back to the Selection mode. You should see the selection marquee around your subject and background edges. The background area around your subject is now selected. To isolate your subject within its own selection, choose Select > Inverse. This reverses your selection.

Create a new layer. Choose Layer > New > Layer Via Copy. This will place a copy of just your subject on a new layer. If your Layers palette is not visible, choose Window > Layers or click the Layers arrow in the palette bin. The Layers palette shows two separate layers: one for the background and another above it that should contain a copy of your subject.

Alter the background. On the Layers palette, click the Background layer to select it. Choose Filter > Blur > Gaussian Blur. Drag the slider until you get an effect you are happy with. Because you have selected only the Background layer, your subject will not be affected. If you are not happy with the results, or if you want to try another filter, choose Edit > Step Backward or Ctrl/Cmd+Z or use the back arrow ().

10 **Save a working version of your photograph.** It's always smart to save a layered working version of your file in case you want to make changes down the road. To save your new version with layers, choose File > Save As, rename the file, and save it in Photoshop format (.psd). If you want to save a single-layer version (commonly known as flattened version), choose File > Save As, rename the file, and deselect the Layers check box. The Save a Copy check box will automatically be selected. Rename your file and save it.

Variation: Experiment with filters

Background with Diffuse Glow filter **Background with Wind filter**

Photoshop Elements has lots of filters and interesting effects. Now that you have your background on a separate layer, you can experiment with them. To see examples of all the filters, choose the Filters tab. When you see a filter you want to try, select it and click Apply.

Variation: Adjust the color of the background

Sometimes it can really be effective to change or remove the color of the background. To do this, choose Image > Enhance > Adjust Color. Then you can choose Hue/Saturation, Replace Color, Remove Color, or Color Variations.

Variation: Use a different image for the background

By now, you are probably realizing that your choices are fairly limitless. You may even be wondering how to go about placing your subject on a whole new background

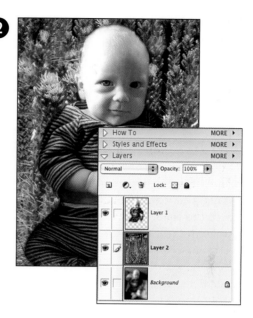

Add a new background image. Open the photo or image that will be used for the new background. (Make sure that your working file is still open and that the Background layer is selected.) Place the two image windows side by side. With your new image active, select the Move tool (⯈₊) from the toolbox. Click the image and drag the new background into your original working file. Note: If the photo bin is open you may either need to close it or choose Window > Cascade in order to see the two files side by side.

Position the new background. Select your working file. On the Layers palette, select your new background layer. Use the Move tool to move it to a position that works with your subject. Save your file.

Project 2

Swap and Add Colors in Your Photographs

Use the painting tools in Photoshop Elements to change or add colors in your photographs.

In this project, you'll learn two different techniques. Working with the Paintbrush tools you'll learn to to add colors to black-and-white images and to replace existing colors in images with completely new ones.

In the first technique we'll show you how to add colors to a either a color or a black-and-white image. This can be used to colorize old photos or just have fun with new ones!

Get started. Open your image in Photoshop Elements.

Remove the current colors. Unless the image you are using is already a black-and-white image, you will want to remove the colors. Choose Enhance > Adjust Color > Remove Color.

Note: If you are working on a black-and-white image, you'll need to change the image mode to one that allows colors. Choose Image > Mode > RGB Color. This will allow you to colorize the image.

Create a new layer. If the Layers palette is not open, click the Layers arrow in the palette bin or choose Window > Layers. Click the New Layer button (▣) at the top of the palette.

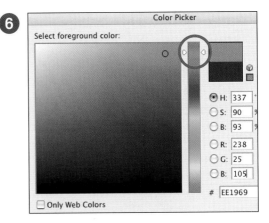

Set layer options. You should always give your layers a descriptive name. This way, even if your file has 50 layers, you can easily identify the one you want. Double-click the new thumbnail to bring up the Layer Properties box. Type *colors* as the layer name.

Next, you will set the layer blending mode. The blending modes are located on the pop-up menu next to the opacity settings on the Layers palette. Click the menu and select Color. This setting will allow the image to show through the color.

Pick your paintbrush. Select the Paintbrush tool (✏) from the toolbox. From the Brushes pop-up menu on the options bar, select a medium-size brush for painting. The brush settings appear on the options bar after you select a brush. Note: The brush size will also depend on the resolution of your image. A medium-size brush for a 300-dpi image will be a large brush for a 72-dpi image.

Choose your paint color. At the bottom of the toolbox, click the Set Foreground Color swatch (🎨). Click in square box to open Color Picker. Use the vertical sliders to find the color area you desire. After you have that set, use the circle to select the exact color you want. Alternatively, choose Window > Color Swatches and click the color you want. You should see the color you've selected in the square in the upper right of the Color Picker box.

7

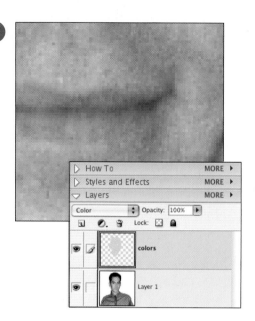

Begin painting. Select your new layer. Zoom in on the area you want to paint. Drag your paintbrush over the area to apply the new color. If you find that your brush is too large, too small, or wrong in some other way, go back to the Brushes menu and select a new brush.

8 **Make corrections.** It happens to the best of us: we make a mistake or change our minds. There are three ways to deal with this. If you just applied the action, press Ctrl/Cmd+Z. If you want to undo more than one step, go to the Undo History palette. This nifty palette allows you to go back 20 steps! The final option to correct a mistake is to use the Eraser tool ( ). The Eraser tool has three forms: Eraser, Background Eraser, and

Magic Eraser. Here, just choose the plain Eraser tool. After you have chosen the eraser mode, you can choose Brush, Pencil, or Block. Choose a setting to complement your current paintbrush and drag over the offending area.

9

Experiment with color. To add more colors, just go back to step 6 and choose a new color.

Create new layers for your new colors and experiment with different layer modes and paintbrushes.

10 **Save a working version.** To save your new version with layers, choose File > Save As, rename the file, and save the file in Photoshop format. If you want to save a single-layer (flattened) version, choose File > Save As, rename the file, and deselect the Layers check box. The Save a Copy check box will automatically be selected. Rename your file and save it.

Variation: Replace existing image colors with completely new ones

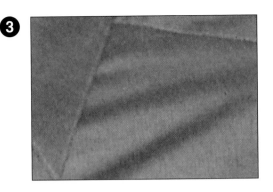

Open your photo.

Set up your brush tool. Choose the Color Replacement brush (🖌), set Limits to contiguous. Set Tolerance to 50-60%.

Sample color to replace. Zoom in and Alt/Option+Click on the color you want to replace.

Choose your color and paint! Use a fairly large soft brush for areas with obvious borders. For areas with a less obvious border or broader color spectrum go back and set a lower tolerance.

Experiment!

CREATE YOUR OWN LOOK!
Try out different Adjustment Layers, like Posterize, to create a whole new look.

HIGHLIGHTS
Create a highlight by hand-painting one object in your image.

Project 3

Create Multiple-Photo Pages

Duplicate your image in multiple sizes for print.

Have you ever had an image that you wanted to make into a holiday card or duplicate for friends and relatives? Here is a quick and easy way to create a multiple-picture layout using just one file.

①

Edit your image. Make all of the necessary edits to the image you want to use. Since you will be printing it, the resolution should be between 150 dpi and 300 dpi depending on how big you want the prints to be. Save a copy of the file. You can also leave the file open if you want.

② **Choose your file.** Choose File > Picture Package. Under Source, do one of the following;

• If your image is still active, select Use Frontmost Document.

• If the image is not still active, navigate to your file on the hard drive and select it.

③

Set layout options. Under Layout, choose a template that will suit your need. Note: Use the **online help** in Photoshop Elements if you want to create a new template or edit an existing one.

④

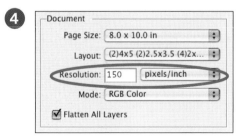

Set the resolution. Enter the final resolution you want for your printed image. If you are uncertain what resolution to choose, enter 150.

Remember that the higher the resolution (dpi), the sharper the image, and the bigger the file size.

Select RGB if your image is in color, and Grayscale if it is in black and white.

5 **Go.** Click OK to create your picture package. When it is done, save the file. Your image is now ready to print!

Variation: Add text automatically

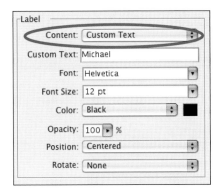

Enter the text. Suppose you want to add a label with the name of your subject and the date that the photo was taken. You can do this in Photoshop Elements using the Text tool (T), but there is an easier way. Go to the Label area located at the bottom of the Picture Package dialog box. In the Custom Text field, enter your text. Proceed through the remaining boxes to customize the font, size, color, and position of the label.

Tools:

Photoshop Elements

(Optional) InDesign

Materials:

Your photos

Templates

Project 4

Create a Contact Sheet for Your Image CD

Easily create thumbnails of all of your images by creating a contact sheet that will fit into any jewel case.

How often have you burned a CD of all of your images but then wanted a quick way to reference them at a glance? The automated contact sheet feature in Photoshop Elements gives you an easy way to do this.

Mac directions

1 **Get started.** Create a folder on your desktop. Place all of the images that you want on the contact sheet in that folder.

2

Choose your source. Choose File > Print Layouts > Contact Sheet. Under Source Images, click Choose and navigate to the folder you created in step 1.

3

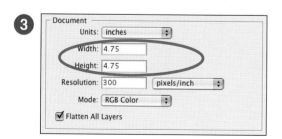

Set up your file. Under Document, type 4.75 for Width and Height. Make sure that the measurement units are set to inches.

For Resolution, type 150 or 300. Even though your images will be quite small, you want to be able to see them clearly. A higher resolution will help.

Choose RGB Color for Mode. If your images are black and white, then choose Grayscale.

4

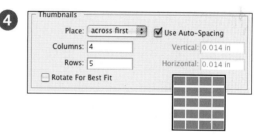

Image layout options. Under Thumbnails, you can specify the number of images that appear on a page and how they are sorted. Click Place and choose Across First or Down First. The Columns and Rows settings determine the size of the thumbnails. Experiment to figure out what works best for you. Your settings will depend on whether your images are horizontal, vertical, square, or rectangular.

Create the reference label. If it is not already checked, select Use Filename as Caption. Photoshop Elements will then label the image with its existing name. Choose a different font and type size if you want. Click OK. Photoshop Elements will then begin placing all of your images into one file. If you have more than will fit on a page, it creates a new file. When the images are all in the file, save and then print your new contact sheet.

PC directions

1 **Get Started.** Open Organizer in Photoshop Elements and create a Collection of the images you want on your contact sheet. (For more information on creating a Collection see Project 17). Double-click your Collection so that you are viewing only those images.

Alternatively, you can Shift-click the images in the Browser window to select which ones you want. This might work well if you don't have too many images.

3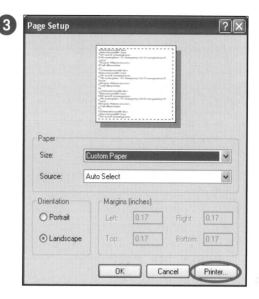

Set your print size. Click Page Setup and choose Printer, then Properties. Under Paper size; choose the preset CD size if it has one or, choose Custom and set the size to 4.75 for both Width and Height.

2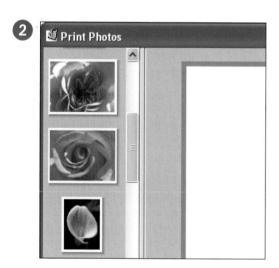

Preview your images. Choose File > Print. All of your images will show in the preview pane on the left side of the Print Photos dialog box.

Select the layout. Click the pop-up menu for Type of Print and choose Contact Sheet.

At this point you will want to set up any other options for your contact sheet such as: date, captions, and page numbers.

5 **You're Done!** Click Print and you're ready to go

Variation: Create a title

Add a title in Photoshop Elements using the Type tool. After Elements has created the contact sheets, there is more you can do. For instance, you might want to title your CD.

To do this, select the Type tool from the toolbox and click on the image, where you want to enter your text. You can always move the text later though, so don't worry if it's not exactly where you want it on the first try.

After choosing the font and size, enter your text for the title. When you have finished, use the Move tool (⨁) to move the title into place.

Once you have your contact sheets, you can go a step further. Using the InDesign templates provided with this project, you can create an actual double-sided booklet that contains your contact sheets and any other information you want to add. The templates are located on the CD in Project folder number 4.

FOLD IT!
This is an example of a folding CD cover.

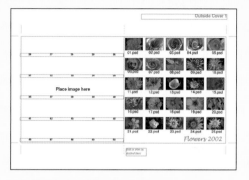

IMPORT YOUR IMAGE
After you have edited the text, place your images. Select the placeholder frame at the right of the first page and choose File > Place. Navigate to your first contact sheet and click Yes. This is now the front cover of your booklet.

Repeat this step if you have more than one contact sheet to place.

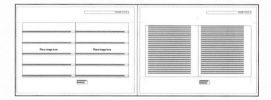

USE THE TEMPLATE
Use InDesign to open the template provided with this project. After you open it, save it with a new name. Notice the placeholders for text and images. To alter the text, select the Type tool, then highlight the template text and enter your own in place of it. If there are unneeded text blocks, simply delete them.

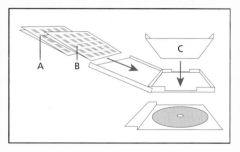

SAVE, PRINT, AND ASSEMBLE
After you have finished creating your layout, save the file; then print and assemble the CD case according the diagram above.

Project 5

Create a Panoramic Image

Let Photoshop Elements automatically create your panoramic image or do it yourself.

This technique is for all those fabulous scenes where your camera lens wasn't quite wide enough. You can use it for long, wide landscapes or even for piecing together the façade of a grand building.

1 **Organize your images.** Once you have all of the images you want to combine, place them in one folder for easy access.

2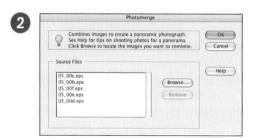

Choose your files. Open Photoshop Elements and choose File > Create > Photomerge. Under Source Files, click Browse and navigate to your folder of images. Select the first image and click Open. You can also select a group of images by holding down the Shift key as you select. You will then see them under Photomerge source files.

3

Merge your images automatically. After you have selected all of your files, click OK. Photoshop Elements will then begin to auto-match your images together. When it is finished, you should see the merged images in the Photomerge dialog box, as in the example above.

4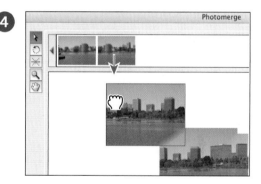

Merge your images manually. Often, Photoshop Elements is unable to place all of your images automatically. When this happens, it will place your images in the thumbnail box above the arranging area. To manually arrange your images, choose the Select Image tool (⬈) from the toolbox and then drag the thumbnail into the arranging area.

⑤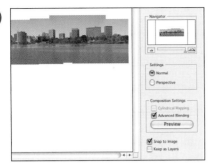

⑥

Set up your options. When your image is selected in the arranging area, you will see a red highlight around it. In the dialog box at the right are all of the options for merging your images together.

To get things started, you may want to turn on Snap to Image. Next, click Perspective to set the vanishing point. Select the Vanishing Point tool from the toolbox and click the image where the vanishing point should be. You will see the images adjust to that perspective. Note: Depending on how your images were shot, you may want to use the Rotate Image tool as well.

Finally, to eliminate any differences in exposure, choose Advanced Blending and click Preview. You may still need to do some touch-up in the final file. If you are happy with the result, click OK. Elements will then create a new file with your combined image.

Edit your new file. Okay, you have your new panoramic image, but it still looks a little less than perfect. Use the Crop tool (⌗) to edit out the ragged edges, and make any other edits the image may need such as adjustments to the color, lighting, and other properties. Choose File > Save As and save your panoramic image with a new name.

Variation: Merging other images

The Photomerge feature doesn't have to be used to create horizontal panoramas. For instance, on your trip through Italy, you may find all sorts of grand church façades, but suppose your camera lens isn't wide enough to capture them? Shoot each part of the façade and then piece it back together using Photomerge.

Once you're done merging the images, click OK to create the new file. Crop and edit the file as needed. Choose File > Save As and save the merged image with a new name.

You may be wondering if there are any good tricks for creating a panorama or other type of merged image. Take a look at the examples here for some tips on how to create seamless, natural-looking merged imagery.

EXPOSURE
Keep the exposure as consistent as possible. This will help you avoid spending time performing lighting and color edits in Photoshop Elements.

RULE OF THIRDS
It's best if your images can overlap by a third (or more). This gives you something to match up.

DON'T MOVE!
Seriously, when you are shooting images that you plan to merge, stay in the same place. This is an instance where you want to, at the very least, keep the same height and perspective. Obviously, if you are shooting architecture, this can't always be done. Just remember: the more angle changes you make, the more finessing you'll need to do with the Perspective tool.

Project 6

Accent Your Photograph
with a Border

Add a finishing touch to your image by using a border.

Placing a border around your photograph is one of the best ways to add a finishing touch. You can either use one of the premade borders shown in the example on the right or create your own by following the instructions. For instructions on using the Cookie Cutter tool to create borders see the Design Tip in Project 8.

1 Get started. Open the photograph or image you want to use in Photoshop Elements.

2 Size your photograph. Using the Crop tool, crop your photograph to 3 inches by 3 inches with a resolution of 200 pixels per inch. See "Use the correct image size" on page 5 for instructions.

After your photograph is resized, you can use any of the borders provided in the project.

3 Select your border. Look through the border templates in the Print folder inside the Proj06 folder. You can also choose one by looking at the examples. Open the template you want to use. Note: Templates P06a.psd through P06d.psd are intended for images that will eventually be placed against a colored background.

If you are planning on using these images for the Web see Variation: Images destined for the Web.

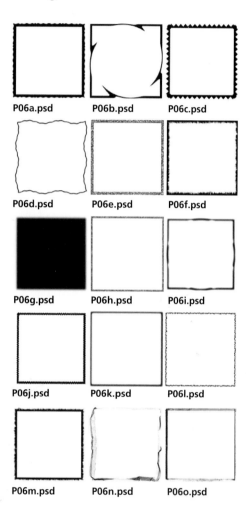

P06a.psd P06b.psd P06c.psd

P06d.psd P06e.psd P06f.psd

P06g.psd P06h.psd P06i.psd

P06j.psd P06k.psd P06l.psd

P06m.psd P06n.psd P06o.psd

④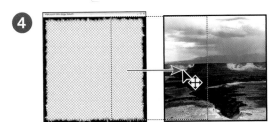

⑤

Place your image within the border.
Make sure that both your photograph
file and border file are open. Place the
image windows side by side to make
them easily accessible. Click your
border to make it active. If you have
the Photo Bin open you need to
choose Window > Cascade to see
both windows.

Select the Move tool (⊕) and place
the cursor in the border. Hold down
the Shift key and drag your border
onto the image. You can release the
mouse after you see the move highlight over the image window. You
have just copied the border around
your image.

Holding down the Shift key while
you drag forces Photoshop Elements
to center your photograph within the
border window. If you didn't hold
down the Shift key, you can always
reposition the border by using the
Move tool again.

Arranging your layers. If you can-
not see your border at this point, this
is because you still need to reposition
the layers. Start by clicking the border
window to make it active. To see
your layers, click the Layers tab in the
palette bin at the top of the screen.
There will be two layers: the border
layer (at the bottom) and your image
layer (on top). To reposition the layers, do one of the following in the
Layers palette:

• Drag the border layer above the
image layer.

• Drag the image layer below the border layer.

You will now see the border around
your photograph.

⑥ **Save a copy of your file.** Save a
copy of your file with the new layers.
Choose File > Save As, rename the
file, and save the file in Photoshop format. If you want to save a single-layer
(flattened) version, choose File > Save
As, rename the file, and deselect the
Layers check box. The Save a Copy
check box is automatically selected.
Rename your file and save it.

Variation: Change the border dimensions

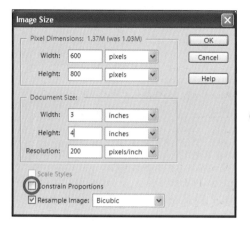

What happens if your image doesn't fit within the border dimensions? No problem; you can still use the borders with a little adjustment.

Simply open the border you want to use and choose Image > Resize > Image Size. Deselect Constrain Proportions box. Set the height and width to values matching your image. Click OK. You can then continue with step 4 to copy your photo into the border window.

Variation: Images destined for the Web

You may be planning on posting your finished images on the Web. If so, you have a couple of options.

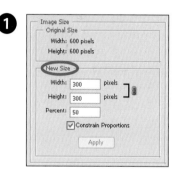

Use for Web. The Save for Web option is the easiest approach if you want to keep a higher-resolution file on hand for printing, but you also want a low-resolution version for the Web. Once you have completed steps 1 through 6, keep the file open and choose File > Save for Web.

In the Save for Web dialog box, enter new size values under New Size. Click Apply.

Choose either GIF or JPEG, depending on what works best with your image.

Note: You can also see how big your file is going to be below the image preview.

When you are satisfied with your settings, click OK and save.

Use a template specified for the Web. If your images are going to be used on the Web only, you may want to use a template set up for the Web. In step 2, set the resolution to 72 pixels per inch. Open a template of your choice located in the Web folder of Project 6 and proceed with steps 3 through 6 of this project.

Variation: Change the borders

Just because you are using a template doesn't mean that you can't give it your own style. One way is to apply some color. This variation works best with templates P06a.psd through P06d.psd, P06f.psd, and P06g.psd (in either the Print or Web folder).

Give the template some color. Choose the color you want to use. Then choose Edit > Fill. Under Contents, choose Foreground Color. Click OK to fill the border with the new color.

Variation: Create your own!

Flex your creativity: Try your hand at creating your own border. One advantage of this approach is that you can add a border without having to resize or crop your original photo.

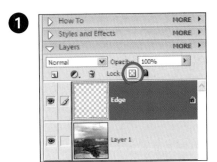

Set up your target layer. After you have rearranged the layers in step 5, select the border layer on the Layers palette and select the Preserve Transparency box on the Layers palette. This will allow you to edit the border without affecting the rest of the layer.

1 **Create a new layer.** Open your photo as in step 1 of the project. Click the Layers tab to bring up the Layers palette.

Then click the New Layer button at the bottom of the palette to add a new layer to your photo.

2 **Set your border.** Click the new layer and choose Select > All or press Ctrl/Cmd+A. This selects the entire layer. Now you need to define the border area. Select the Rectangular Marquee tool (▢). Hold down the Alt/Option key and drag in the interior area of the photo that you want framed by the border. Note: You can use the Elliptical Marquee tool as well. To reposition the selection as you draw, press the spacebar and drag with the Alt/Option key still pressed.

When you hold down the Alt/Option key, the interior area is subtracted from the selection, leaving just the border area selected.

3 **Fill the selection.** Choose a color and then choose Edit > Fill. Under Contents, choose Foreground Color. Alternately, select the Paint Bucket tool (◇)and click the selected area.

4 **Experiment!** Photoshop Elements ships with all sorts of filters. Click the Filters tab to see examples of them. When you see one you want to try, double-click it to apply it to your layer.

A little border can go a long way. Try to avoid borders that are so overly colorful, large, or complex that they overtake the photograph. Here are a couple of tips to keep in mind when creating borders.

When you create your border, remember that the attention is supposed to be on the image, not the border. Make sure that the size and colors are appropriate for the image.

If you will be placing the photo in some sort of publication, you don't need to add a keyline around the photo. Your image has a stylized border already, so you won't want another one.

STYLES

Choose a border style that matches your subject matter. For example, ornate borders can often be used with images of historical or traditional content, while a contemporary border like the Polaroid transfer look of P06b.psd can work with an offbeat image.

WINDOWS only

Using the Creation feature in Photoshop Elements for Windows you can make scrapbooks, cards, and slideshows in a snap. If you want a more customized look, add a border to your images before using them in a Creation.

For more information on using the new Creation feature see Project 16: Create Calendars, Cards and Scrapbooks using Creations.

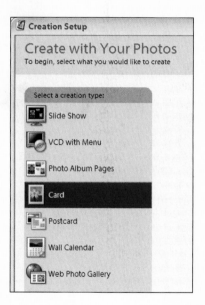

Tools:

Photoshop Elements
InDesign (Optional)

Materials:

Newsletter template
Your photos

Project 7

Publish Your Photographs in a Newsletter

Get your color photos ready for black-and-white or one-color reproduction.

East Bay Athlete

Summer Edition

THE BAYS ONLY CLUB FOR TRI ATHLETES

Articles

Do the shoes make the runner?

Cold water classics

The Competitive edge

Contact Us at ebaytriathlete.com

New Director

Babs Gaston takes over as the club's swim director

Babs Gaston, 4 time winner of the cold water swim accepted the nomination as the club's new swim director. Babs has been active with the club since 2000

in such roles as relay advisor, running consultant and bike race coordinator. Babs has big new plans for swim team over the next year which she will unveil on the Memorial day weekend kickoff. In a recent interview she gave a sneak preview of some of her goals. They include new pool facilities, along with a new team logo and swimwear. Ms Gaston is also planning on adding 5 new races to the team's roster to spice up the year.

Originally from Arizona, Babs has lived all over the continent and has competed in just about every body of water you can think of. Brushes with the wildlife include a shark encounter in 1997 where she narrowly escaped losing her foot to a shark in an open water swim off the Great Barrier Reef. Fortunately there was surgeon convention in town so Ms Gaston still has all her toes.

Volunteers break out the suncreen

All sorts of outdoor activities are lined up for the club this summer, so if you had better buy the bulk size of spf 45 sunscreen. Just some of the things to do include; Relays racing in the park, fund rasing picnics, and all day swim meets at the lake. For more information on what will be happening go to the back page. There is a full listing.

Clear victory in Saturday's race

You can also check out photos of past summer events on our website. If you have some more ideas

or would like to volunteer your time or know some who would please contact us at 510 5551212. Volunteering can mean anything from handing out sliced oranges and stuffing envelopes to blowing ballons. You name it, if you have a special talent for say foot massages those are appreciated too.

Just give us a call and let us know your schedule and we will be sure to fill it up.

Let's say you're putting together a short newsletter for work, school, or a holiday family update. More than likely, it will be printed in black and white. This project gives you the steps to get your image ready.

When you are done editing your image, you can place it in the page layout program of your choice. We've included a newsletter template that you can use if you have a copy of Adobe InDesign CS, but it's not required for this project.

2

Open your photo. Open your first photograph in Photoshop Elements. Take a hard look at it. Are there distractions that could be taken out? Do you want to zoom in on just one person?

1

Get started. You should decide what photos you want to use and what the final printed size will be. Check the resolution of your images. The resolution should be at least 300 pixels per inch.

3

Trim and size the image. Select the Crop tool (⊣) to trim your image to the correct dimensions. Use the options bar to set the exact image size. If the entire image needs to be smaller, choose Image > Image size and enter the dimensions.

If you are going to use the optional InDesign template, use the following image dimensions for the front page: 2.65 inches wide by 2.65 inches high for the first image, and 1.69 inches wide by 1.69 inches high for the second image.

Remove the color. To convert your image to grayscale, choose Image > Mode > Grayscale and click OK. (Remember that it's always a good idea to save a backup version in color before converting your image.)

Adjust the contrast and sharpen. You may notice a loss of contrast and tonal range when converting from color to grayscale. If this is the case, choose Enhance > Adjust Lighting Levels. Drag the triangular sliders under Input Levels to adjust the tonal range. Make sure the Preview box is checked so you can see what is happening to your image. (For more information on levels, refer to online help.)

Finally, to make your image a little snappier, choose Filter > Sharpen > Unsharp Mask. Drag the Amount slider until you are satisfied with the result. Remember to look at detailed areas such as hair, eyes, and foliage. These areas will often benefit from sharpening. Also remember that too much sharpening is not good for smooth areas such as skin tones or blue skies, which tend to become grainy.

Save in TIFF format. One of the widely used printing formats is TIFF. To save your document as a TIFF file, choose File > Save As and save your changes in TIFF format. Make sure you also save the original version.

You are now ready to place your image in InDesign or any other layout software. To use the provided template, open InDesign and then open template P07.t7, located in the Project 7 folder.

Variation: Add a little color

Here is a great technique if you are printing on a personal color printer and want an image with a certain hue: for example, if you are going to print a head shot, and you want it to have a warm sepia tone.

Note: If you are using a professional printer and want to add a color, the image will be called a duotone, and the printer will set it up for you.

Remove the color. In this process, your image will stay in RGB mode; however, you still need to remove the color. To do this, choose Enhance > Adjust Color > Remove Color.

2 **Add back one color.** In this next step, you will be working with an adjustment layer. Adjustment layers provide a marvelous way to apply edits to your image that are nondestructive—which means that you can go back and change the edits at any time.

Click the Layers arrow to open the Layers palette. Click the Adjustment Layers icon (⦿) located at the top of the palette. Choose Hue/Saturation.

Adjust the hue. First, make sure the Colorize box is checked. Then drag the Hue slider until you see your desired color. Experiment with the saturation of the color by dragging the Saturation slider. When you are satisfied with the result, click OK. If you want to change the settings later, double-click the layer thumbnail on the Layers palette.

4 **Save an export version.** Again, save the original; then choose File > Save As, rename the file, and save the file in TIFF format.

3

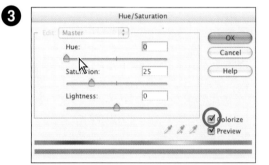

Grayscale

Red Hue

Cyan Hue

Yellow Hue

When using a page layout program such as InDesign, you can choose an accent color for text, graphics, and images. If you go to a print shop, this will be called a spot color. This process is most commonly referred to as printing a duotone. In choosing your spot color, you should select a color that will work in a variety of tint percentages or shades. Here are some good tips for working with color.

SPOT COLORS
A sign of a good spot color is that it works well with reverse type.

100%	■ type	■ type	■ type
85%	■ type	■ type	■ type
70%	■ type	■ type	■ type
55%	■ type	■ type	■ type
40%	■ type	■ type	■ type
25%	■ type	■ type	■ type
10%		■ type	■ type

WORKS FOR EVERYTHING
Your color needs to be dark enough to be used for type as well as for photos.

100%	■ type	■ type	■ type
85%	■ type	■ type	■ type
70%	■ type	■ type	■ type
55%	■ type	■ type	■ type
40%	■ type	■ type	■ type
25%	■ type	■ type	■ type
10%			

BEWARE
Light colors such as yellow, orange, and cyan can disappear at tints of less than 80 percent.

Project 8

Create Postcards and Posters

Create great postcards and posters using your own photographs or just Photoshop Elements for your artwork.

This project can be used in a variety of ways. Let's say you want to create a simple postcard for a friend's party. Easy enough: you can either create one from one of the templates provided or create one by combining an image of your choice with one of the templates. Or let's say you have a two-year old and want to create a birthday party announcement. You'll want to create a fun postcard and poster that gives all the pertinent information. You can do that, too.

1 **Get ready.** First, decide if you are going to use a template that calls for your own photograph or one of the template textures. If you are going to use your own photograph, make sure the resolution and size of the image match the resolution and size of the template being used. If you are creating more than one piece, such as a postcard and a poster, you can use the larger image for both pieces.

Open the template you are going to use from the Proj08 folder. Choose File > Save As and save the file with a new name. If you want a double-sided postcard, you will need to open both post_#a and post_#b to create the front and back sides.

Use the postcard gallery to help you decide which template to use. Each postcard has accompanying templates for a flyer and a poster.

P08b1_a.psd

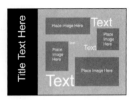

P08b2_a.psd

P08b1&2 b.psd

P08b3_a.psd

P08b3_b.psd

P08b4_a.psd

P08b4_b.psd

②

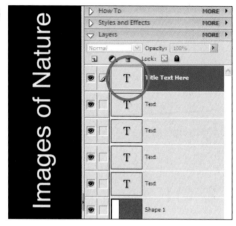

Change the typeface. You will probably want to change the font of the title to match the style of your photo. To change the font, with the text still selected, choose a new font from the options bar pull-down menu. You can adjust the size at the same time.

Edit the template. This example uses the postcard template P08b2_a.psd. To edit the type, bring up the Layers palette by clicking the Layers arrow in the palette bin.

Double-click the title text layer to select the type. Enter your own text.

④

③

Color your type. Double-click the 'T' icon in the layers palette to select your text if it is not still selected, then click the Color swatch on the options bar. Or to choose more colors, go to Color Picker and select the perfect hue. If you want, you can use the Eyedropper tool to pick up a color from your image. The pointer will change to the Eyedropper tool ( ) when it's outside the Color Picker.

Repeat steps 2, 3, and 4 for any other type layers that may be in the template you are using.

⑤

Images of Nature

⑥

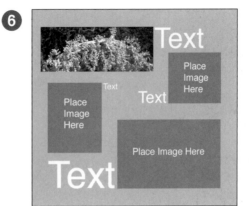

Shape changes. Depending on the template you are using, there may be some shape layers that you want to alter. For instance, you may want to change the color of the shape layer under the text, as in this example. To change the color of a shape layer, simply double-click the shape layer on the Layers palette. This brings up the Color dialog box. From here, you can either choose a color from the Color Picker or use the Eyedropper tool to pick up a color from the image.

Note: This is also a good place to use the Cookie Cutter tool, which allows you to cut out shapes of images or color filled layers. For more information on using the Cookie Cutter tool see the design tip in Project 9.

Place your photo. Select the place-holder image layer on the postcard template so that when you place your image, it will be in the proper layer order. Open the image you are going to use in Photoshop Elements. If you have not done so already, check the resolution and size of your image to make sure they match the template. For more information on cropping and image resizing, see "Use the correct image size" on page 5.

Position the template window next to your image window or in a way that you can view both windows. If the Photo Bin is open you may need to Choose Window > Cascade to do this. Click the image window to make it active. Select the Move tool (▸₊) and place the cursor inside the image. Click the image and drag it into the postcard file.

Alternately, select your image and choose Select > All or Ctrl/Cmd+A from the menu bar and then Edit > Copy. Select the postcard file and choose Edit > Paste or Ctrl/Cmd+V.

7 Scale your photo. If your photo is too large, choose Image > Transform > Free Transform. Hold down the Shift key and drag inward on a corner box. Holding down Shift ensures that your photo will stay in proportion. Hit Return or Enter.

8 Delete placeholders. When you are finished adding images, delete any remaining placeholder layers. Select the layer and turn off the eye icon, or click the trash icon on the Layers palette.

9

Add some final style. The Styles and Effects palette in Photoshop Elements allows you to add drop shadows, bevels, textures, and patterns to your layer.

To apply a style to your text, click the text layer, and then click the arrow in the Styles and Effects tab.

On the Styles and Effects palette, select Layer Styles under the first pop-up menu, then select one of the options under the second pop-up. Experiment with combining some of the style options, such as a drop shadow with a pattern. To clear a style, click Remove Style. To adjust any of the effects on your layer, choose from Layer Styles.

10

Copy title effects to your photos. You may want to apply the same effects that you applied to your text to your images. Select the layer with the effect you want to copy. Next, select the text layer in the menu bar. Choose Layer Effects > Copy Layer Style. Next, select the image layer and choose Layer > Layer Effects > Paste Layer Style.

11 **Save and print your card or poster.**
Remember: You always want to save
a working version of your file. Choose
File > Save As and save the file with a
new name. To print your file, choose
File > Save As and select the Save a
Copy box. Choose TIFF as your file
format and save the file with a new
name. You are almost ready to print.

To make life a little easier, Photoshop
Elements has a feature that will print
crop marks. This saves you the time
of adding them afterward so that you
can trim your printout. To set this
up, choose File > Print to see print
preview and click the Show More
Options box. Select the Crop Marks
box. You can also specify a border size
by clicking Border. You are now ready
to print.

If you are printing multiple postcards
and would like to save some paper,
see Project 3, which describes how
to create multiple layouts.

If you have created a double-sided
postcard, you should have two files.
Unless you are going to use a professional printer, you will need to feed
your card stock back through your
printer to print the back side.

For tips on card stocks to use see
"Choose paper for postcards" on
page 59.

Variation: Create textures

With a little experimentation, you can
create your own textures in Photoshop Elements either from scratch or
by using a photo. They can be used to
complement your images or replace
the textures in the templates.

1 **Set the stage.** Open Photoshop
Elements and create a new file the
size of the template you will be using.
If you are using an image, place the
image in the new file and move to step
3. If you are working from scratch, go
to step 2.

2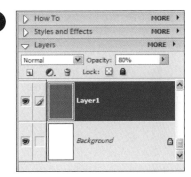

Pick a color. First create a new layer.
Click the Layers tab in the docking
area to bring up the Layers palette.
Click the New Layer icon (▣) and
select the new layer that is created.
Click the Default Colors icon (▰)
and pick a new color using the Color
Picker. Choose Edit > Fill Layer.
Under Contents, select Use Fore-
ground Color. Click OK.

3

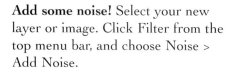

4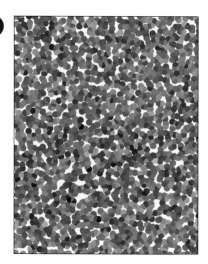

Add some noise! Select your new layer or image. Click Filter from the top menu bar, and choose Noise > Add Noise.

If you are starting with an image, this step is optional, but if you are starting from scratch, it's a must. Double-click the Add Noise filter and make sure that the Preview box is checked.

Experiment with the settings. This example uses the default Amount setting and the Gaussian distribution. The Monochromatic setting is turned off to get more colors in the mix. Make your own choices; then click OK when you are satisfied.

Use those filters. It's not always easy to use the filters in everyday image correction. When you are creating textures, however, they are absolutely essential.

Grant yourself full license to go crazy and experiment with various combinations of filters to see what you like and what works best. The example here uses Colored Pencil and Pointillize. When you have finished creating your new texture, choose File > Save As and save your file with a new name in a TIFF format. It is now ready to be placed in the template of your choice.

Before printing your postcard, you will want to think about your paper thickness and texture. The minimum thickness you can use for mailing a stand-alone card is 7 points. Most 7-point stock is uncoated, meaning not glossy. You will also need to think about what can go through your printer unless you are using a professional printing house.

The other option for postcards is an 8-point stock coated on one side (commonly referred to as 8-point C1S). The advantage to using a card stock that is glossy on one side is that the image will look good, and you can still write on the other side.

Paper stock that is coated on one side comes in thicknesses of 8, 10, 12, and 14 points. You should run a test sheet through your printer if you are printing at home. You can find heavier stock, but it is often too heavy to use in many printers (even professional ones).

Tools:

Photoshop Elements

Materials:

Phototransfer paper

Your image & fabric

Templates

Project 9

Create Stickers, T-shirts, Tattoos, and More!

Use the project templates and phototransfer paper to place images on T-shirts, magnets, and more.

Your local big office supply store has a huge variety of transfers that allow you to put your art/images/photos onto T-shirts, postcards, greeting cards, door hangers, labels, bumper stickers, tattoos, or just plain old photographic paper. This allows you to put any image you can create in Elements onto practically any surface. The possibilities are endless!

Have you wanted to create your own T-shirt design, maybe for a sports team or special event? This project gives you the templates for adding images, logos, and slogans to T-shirts and other items. All you need are your images and ideas.

1 **Check the size of your artwork.** Depending on what you're creating, you may have a few different types of files. For example, if you are creating something for a sports team, you may have logo artwork, or you may be using your new baby's photograph on a tote bag for grandma.

In either case, the logo or image dimensions need to be approximately 6 x 9 inches with a resolution of 150 pixels per inch. The exact dimensions will vary depending on the template you use, so look at the template size first. To check the resolution and size of your image in Photoshop Elements, choose Image > Resize > Image Size. For more information see "Use the correct image size" on page 5.

Artwork that is vector based, such as an Adobe Illustrator file, can be resized inside the template.

2

Edit your photograph. Open the photograph that you want to use in Photoshop Elements. Make any color corrections and other edits that the photo may need.

3 **Save two versions.** After you have finished making edits to your image, choose File > Save As. Rename the file and save it in a Photoshop format. This will save any layers in the file in case you want to make changes later.

Next, choose File > Save As and select TIFF as the format, making sure to deselect the Layers option box.

Save the file with the .tif suffix so you don't replace the working version. Close the file.

P09a.psd

P09b.psd

P09d.psd

P09c.psd

P09e.psd

P09f.psd

Edit the template.
In the Project 9 folder, open the template that you want to use in Photoshop Elements and save it with a new name. If the Layers palette is not visible, click the Layers arrow in the palette bin. Notice that there is a text layer for a slogan or company saying on the Layers palette.

Double-click the text layer to select the text. Enter your own message or company slogan. Change the font and size using the pop-up menus on the Type options bar. To change the color of the text, click the color swatch on the Type options bar. Select a new color using the Color Picker that appears; then click OK. For information on editing template colors and image masks, see Projects 8 and 11.

Place and size your artwork. Use one of the following techniques to place your artwork.

Select the *place image here* layer. This is important because this will position your image below the layer mask.

• Choose Select > All or Ctrl/Cmd+A. Then select Edit > Copy or Ctrl/Cmd+C, then go back to your template file choose Edit > Paste or Ctrl/Cmd+V.

• For vector artwork such as logos: Choose File > Place. Navigate to your file and select Place. Use the handles to resize the image after it is placed in the template. After you place the artwork, use the Move tool to position it.

6 **Save and print your file.** Repeat step 3 and save two versions of the new file: one Photoshop version and one TIFF version for printing. After saving the file, choose File > Print to print your file on phototransfer paper. Note: Different manufacturers of phototransfer papers have different printing setup requirements. Follow the manufacturer's instructions.

Use the Cookie Cutter tool to create your own design. You can use it on a picture or a layer that has been filled with a color.

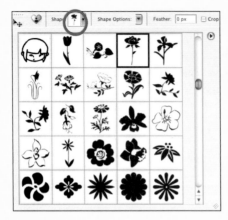

SELECT YOUR SHAPE
Open your image in Photoshop Elements. Choose the Cookie Cutter tool from the toolbox ( ). Select the Shape pop-up palette from the options bar and click on the shape you want. (For more shapes click the pop-up button on the palette and choose All Element Shapes.)

CREATE YOUR FINAL IMAGE!
Click on your chosen shape and drag it over the image. (Remember to hold down the Shift key to constrain proportions.) Press Enter/Return to apply the shape.

Note: If you don't like the effect either press the back arrow or Ctrl/Cmd+Z to go back.

Printing a mirror image

Read the detailed instructions that come with the phototransfer paper. Most papers work from a mirror image so that the image and text will be correct when ironed onto a fabric. If your printer does not have a mirror or reverse setting, use the following steps to create a mirror image.

1   In your TIFF file, choose Image > Rotate > Flip Horizontal.

2   Choose File > Print and print according to the instructions of the paper manufacturer.

Prepping the fabric

○ Prewash the material to remove any residual chemicals.

○ Rinse clean with no softeners or additives.

Ironing

○ Preheat the iron using the highest setting and drain any water from steam irons.

○ A normal ironing board is too soft so use a low, hard surface such as a counter or table at waist or knee level. This allows you to lean over the iron and exert strong pressure along with the high heat.
DO NOT USE A GLASS TABLE!

○ Place a wrinkle-free pillowcase on the ironing surface. Center the transfer area of your fabric over the pillowcase.

Tools:

Photoshop Elements

Materials:

Cover templates for CDs,
binders, and videos

Your photos

Project 10

Blend Multiple Images to Create Covers for CDs, Binders, and More

Give your covers a striking look by blending imagery, text, and graphics.

Have you ever seen a collage of images that, pieced together, meant more than each image separately? Such a grouping is often used to tell a story or to make a visual connection for the viewer.

In this project, you will blend two separate images together to create one illustration. You will then combine this image with text and graphics to create a cover for a CD, binder, or video.

① **Get started.** Open the Photoshop Elements template that you want to use for the project. There are three types of templates: for a CD cover, a binder cover, and a video cover. They are located in the Project 10 folder. After you have opened your template, open the images you plan to blend together.

②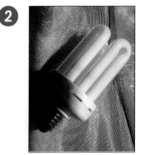

Size your images. Look at the template file to determine the exact resolution and dimensions for your images. The resolution needs to be the same for both images. For tips on image resizing and resolution, see "Use the correct image size" on page 5.

③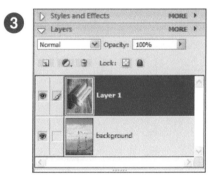

Copy and paste. Click the image you want in the foreground of your illustration and choose Select > All or Ctrl/Cmd+A to select everything; then choose Edit > Copy or Ctrl/Cmd+C. At this point, you can close the file.

Select the background image and choose Edit > Paste or Ctrl/Cmd+V. You now have two separate layers in your file, each containing one image. To see your Layers palette, click the Layers arrow in the palette bin. You may want to keep this palette open so you can always see what is happening.

④ Save a backup version. As always, you should have a working file that contains all of your layers. Choose File > Save As and save your work in a new file with a different name in Photoshop format. This ensures that you can always go back to your original work and make new edits.

⑤

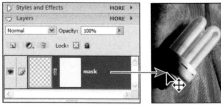

Import a new layer with a mask. You will now import a new empty top layer with a layer mask. The layer mask will be the agent for blending the two layers. Follow these steps:

• In the menu bar choose Window > Images > Cascade. This will allow you see the files next to each other.

• Open the mask.psd file located in the project folder.

• Click the mask layer inside the Layers palette and drag to the image file you want to blend.

You should now see the new empty layer at the top of your Layers palette. The empty box you see next to it is the layer mask that you will be working with in step 7.

⑥

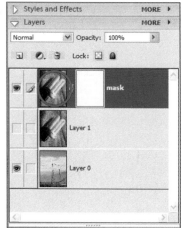

Add the image to your new layer.

• Click on your top image layer to select it. Choose Select > All or Ctrl/Cmd+A.

• Choose Edit > Copy or Ctrl/Cmd+C.

• Select the empty layer.

• Choose Edit > Paste Into Selection or Shift-Ctrl/Cmd+V.

Hide the original top image layer by clicking the eye icon next to it.

Create the blend of two images. You next need to paint in the layer mask so the bottom layer can show through. This can be done in a variety of ways, but here you will use the Gradient tool. For other methods, see the variations at the end of the project.

First, click the layer mask on the Layers palette. A little mask icon () appears next to the eye icon on the palette. This lets you know that you are working in the mask and not in the image.

Choose the Gradient tool (▭) from the toolbox. On the options bar, click the gradient picker to choose a gradient. Select the default black-to-white or black-to-transparent gradient. A mask can only be in grayscale. Wherever black is applied in the image mask, the image will be hidden, and the opposite is true for white. By using a gradient, you are creating a soft blend of the two images.

The default gradient type is Linear. This is a good type to start with. Place the cursor on one side of the image and then drag to the other side.

Adjusting the amount or angle of the blend is easy. Just make sure that your mask is selected and then drag with the Gradient tool from different areas of the image until you are satisfied with the results. Experiment with other types of gradients such as Radial, Reflected, and Diamond.

Choose File > Save.

8

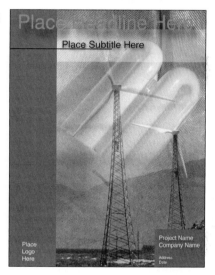

Place the image in the template. Make sure that your top layer is selected. Choose Select > All or Ctrl/Cmd+A and then Edit > Copy Merged. Click the template that you opened at the beginning of the project to make it active. Select the bottom layer and choose Edit > Paste or Ctrl/Cmd+V.

⑨

Place Headline Here

Place Subtitle Here

Add your text. Double-click the Title layer; the text should be selected. Enter your own title. Repeat this process for any other text layers in the template. If there is text that you don't want, click the eye icon next to it to hide it. To move the title or any other text, select the Move tool (⊕) and drag the text to the position you want.

⑩

Renewable Energy

Wind Power: The Next Big Thing?

Alternative Energy
Green Power

645 Park Blvd.
Oakland, CA
June 2, 2003

Adjust colors and styles. You will probably want to change the color of the shapes or text to match your image better. To change the color of the text, select the Text tool (T) and click the text layer. Then click the color swatch on the options bar, or use the Color Picker to choose a new color for your text.

Changing the color of a shape is just as easy. Just double-click the shape layer and use the color picker to choose your color.

⑪ Save working and export versions of the image. Save your working file. Then choose File > Save a Copy, rename the file, and save it in TIFF format, making sure to deselect the Layers option box.

Variation: Select creatively

A. No mask

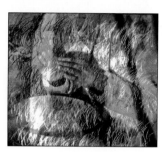

B. Using the Leaf Brush

Make creative selections. You don't have to use the regular Marquee tool to make your selection. Try using the selection brush and experiment with different brushes. Remember that when you are using the Paintbrush tool, black adds to the mask, and white takes away from the mask.

Variation: Change modes

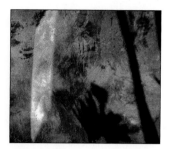

A. No mask

B. Screen mode

Try a new mode. It can also be fun to experiment with different Layer modes.

Blending images can be a tricky process. Often, it's good to work with one image that creates more of a pattern and one that is the focal point. How you treat your text and titles can greatly affect the final image as well

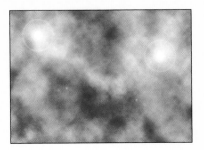

OPPOSITES DO ATTRACT!
When blending images, it often works well to have one of the images be more of a texture or more abstract than the other.

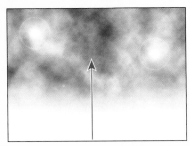

A GRADUAL PROCESS
In this example, a linear gradient works well to create a gradual blend with the image below.

THE RIGHT TYPE
This friendly script works well with the subject matter of organic food.

Tools:

Photoshop Elements

InDesign

Materials:

Mask templates

Ad template

Your photo

Project 11

Create a Black-and-White Ad for Publication

Create a professional advertisement for use in a black-and-white publication.

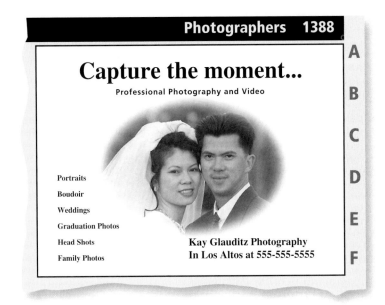

You can use Photoshop Elements to create your own advertisements. In this project, you will use a template to create a typical ad that can be used in a black-and-white publication. All you need is your own photo; the template provides the mask and text block. Note: The CD contains an optional InDesign template that can be used for placing text.

1 **Get started.** Open your image in Photoshop Elements.

Trim and resize the photo. For the purposes of this template, the photograph needs to be 130 points high and 175 points wide, with a resolution of 144 pixels per inch (for more information see "Use the correct image size" on page 5).

Make the photo black and white. Choose Image > Mode > Grayscale and then click OK.

You may notice a loss of contrast and tonal range going from color to grayscale. If this is the case, choose Enhance > Adjust Lighting > Levels. Drag the triangular sliders under Input Levels to adjust the tonal range. Make sure the Preview box is checked so you can see what is happening to your image.

(For more information on levels, refer to the Photoshop Elements online help.)

④

⑤

Place your photo in the template.
Open one of the templates in the Proj11 folder. (Use P11a.psd for an oval photo, and P11b.psd for a rectangular photo.) The illustration here shows the drag-and-drop technique. To use this technique, arrange the image and template windows so that you can see both of them at the same time. If the Photo Bin is open you may need to go to Window > Images > Cascade or Tile in order to see your images side by side.

Select the Move tool (⯈₊) and Shift-drag your photo into the mask template. Release the mouse when the template window becomes highlighted. This technique places a centered copy of your image in the template. You can also copy and paste your image into the template "mask template."

Select the mask. If it is not already visible, bring up the Layers palette by clicking the Layers arrow in the palette bin. On the Layers palette, Ctrl/Cmd+click the Oval or Rectangle layer to select the mask shape. To stop the "marching ants" press Ctrl/Cmd+D, which deselects the image.

6

Subtract the mask shape from your image. You are going to delete the mask shape from your image, but first you need to feather the edge of your selection. Select your photo layer in the Layers palette and then choose Select > Feather, enter 8 to create a nice soft edge, and click OK.

Press Delete or Backspace to delete the selection from the photo. Hide the Oval or Rectangle layer by clicking the eye icon on the Layers palette. As you can see, feathering the selection gives a softer edge to the selection outline.

7 **Save two versions of your file.** Remember to always save a working version of your file that contains all of your layers. To do this, choose File > Save As, rename the file, and save it in Photoshop format. Next, save a flattened (no layers) version for export. Choose File > Save As, check the Save a Copy box, and save the file in TIFF format with a new name. Be sure to deselect the Layers option box.

You can now use the TIFF version in either the Elements ad template or the InDesign ad template. The following steps assume that you are using the template in Photoshop Elements.

8

Choose your template. There are three ad layout templates in Photoshop Elements: P11c, d, and e. Open the one you want to use along with the TIFF file you just saved. Note: If you have the Photo Bin open you may need to choose Window > Images > Cascade from the menu bar in order to view your images side by side.

Your headline here
Supporting line

List of
services
or products
Item A
Item B
Item C

Company Name/Logo
City • voice 555-555-5555

Capture the moment...
Professional Photography and Video

Portraits
Boudoir
Weddings
Graduation Photo
Head Shots
Family Photos

Company Name/Logo
City • voice 555-555-5555

Place your new photograph. Arrange the two files so that you see both of them. Using the drag-and-drop technique that you used earlier, place the TIFF file in the template.

Replace the text with your own. Double-click the text layers to select the text and enter your own copy. You can change the fonts on the text options bar to match the style of your ad.

Again, save a working version with all of the layers in case you want to make any changes later. After you have a working version saved, save your file in TIFF format using a different name. Be sure to deselect the layers option.

Have you ever noticed how some advertisements really jump off the page: Did you immediately know who the target customer was? Was it visually striking and compelling? These are some questions you want your own audience to answer yes to when you are creating an advertisement for any type of promotional purpose. The following tips offer some good advice for creating effective ads.

KEEP IT BRIEF
A short, strong headline captures the attention of your customers and makes them interested in what you have to say.

MAKE A CHANGE
Use a different font to highlight critical points,

LESS IS MORE
Try to avoid a cluttered image. White space gives the message more impact.

USE STRONG IMAGERY
It's best not to use a photo that has too much going on.

Project 12

Create Photographic Backgrounds
and Sidebars for Slide Presentations

*Make your next presentation more exciting by using Photoshop Elements
to create photographic backdrops and sidebars.*

This project is for you presentation artists who want to expand beyond the usual templates and bullet points that come with slide presentations. Photographic backgrounds can put your presentation text into a context—something your audience, whether they know it or not, will appreciate. Photographic sidebars can give your presentation a visual frame that places the main text, graphs, or charts within a context. The center of the slide remains available for informational content, with the photograph seen only on the edges. Using the provided sidebar templates, you can create numerous photographic effects for online slides.

In part 1 of this project, you will learn how to create a photographic background. In part 2 you will learn how to create a photographic sidebar using one of the templates.

For a final touch, look at Project 13 to find out how you can create a PDF slideshow right in Photoshop Elements.

① **Part 1: Get started.** Open the photograph you want to use for a slide background in Photoshop Elements.

② **Trim and size the photo.** Use the Crop tool to resize the photo to a height of 480 pixels and a width of 640 pixels. The resolution should be 72 pixels per inch (see "Use the correct image size" on page 5). These dimensions will allow you to produce a full-screen display for monitors and online projectors. If you work with an outside vendor to create or output your slides, check to find out the size the vendor uses.

③ **Create a new shape.** If it's not already visible, open the Layers palette by clicking the Layers arrow in the palette bin.

Select the Rectangle shape tool (▣) from the toolbox and drag inside the image. Don't worry about the color just yet.

This rectangle is going to become a semitransparent shape over the image area in which you will place your text. Note: Feel free to choose other shapes if you want to experiment.

Here are some quick shortcuts to transform, rotate, or distort a shape.

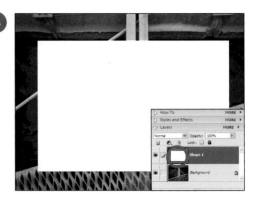

- To scale and center the shape layer, hold down Alt/Option and drag a handle.

- To rotate the shape, place the pointer outside the bounding box and drag in the direction you want to rotate.

- To distort freely, press Ctrl/Cmd and drag a handle.

- To skew, press Ctrl/Cmd+Shift and drag a side handle.

- To apply perspective, press Ctrl+Alt+Shift/Cmd+Option+Shift and drag a corner handle.

- To undo the last change, choose Edit > Undo or use the Back arrow.

Press Enter to apply the transformation or Esc to cancel the transformation.

Change the shape color. To change the color of your shape layer, double-click the shape on the Layers palette. Choose white from the Color Picker.

To choose a color from your image, simply move your cursor from the Color Picker into the image area. This will give you the Eyedropper tool. Click to sample a color in the image; then click OK.

⑤

Variation: Soften the edges

Screen back the layer. Make sure that your shape layer is selected on the Layers palette. Using the opacity slider, change the opacity setting to 50%. You can also experiment with layer modes for different effects.

⑥ Save two versions. As always, save a working version of your file that contains all of your new layers. This will allow you to easily go back and make adjustments and changes if you need to. To use the file in another program, you will want a single-layer version. Choose File > Save As and select the Save a Copy check box. Under Format, choose TIFF or a format supported by your presentation application; then save the file with a new name. Note: Make sure the Layers check box is deselected.

If the look you are after is a more gradual edge, then use this technique.

Select your shape layer and choose Filter > Blur > Gaussian Blur. A dialog box will appear telling you that the layer needs to be simplified for this filter. Once this is done your layer will be changed from vector to pixel based.

Click OK and proceed to the next dialog box to create your Gaussian Blur.

1 **Part 2: Get started.** Open your photo file in Photoshop Elements; then open the templates sidebar you want to use. The Proj12 folder contains eight templates, each with a different sidebar shape and layout.

P12a.psd

P12b.psd

P12c.psd

P12d.psd

P12e.psd

P12f.psd

P12g.psd

P12h.psd

2 **Size the photo.** To use these templates, you will need to crop and resize the photo to at least 480 pixels high or 640 pixels wide at 72 pixels per inch, same as before. (See "Use the correct image size" on page 5).

3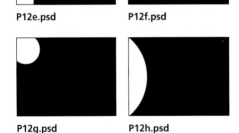

Place the photo in the template. Arrange the photo and template windows side by side, or so that you can see both of them. Click the photo window to make it active and then select the Move tool (⬆). Note: If the Photo Bin is open, you can either close it, or choose Window > Images > Cascade to see more than one document at a time.

Use the Move tool to drag the photo into the sidebar template. When a highlight appears around the template window, release the mouse button. This will drop a copy of the photo into the template window. You can reposition the photo in the template by dragging it with the Move tool.

4

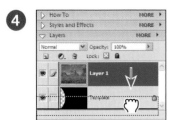

Arrange the layers. If your Layers palette is not open, click the Layers arrow in the palette bin. On the Layers palette, drag the photo layer to the bottom of the list.

5

Select a color for the slide. Select the Eyedropper tool ( ) from the toolbox and click in the photo to sample a color for the body of the slide. The sampled color will appear in the Foreground color swatch ( ).

6

Color the slide body. Select the Template layer on the Layers palette, and choose Edit > Fill. When the dialog box appears, choose Foreground Color for the contents; then click OK.

7 **Save two versions of the file.** It's always a good idea to save a working version of your file in case you want to make changes. To save a working version with all of the layers, choose File > Save As, rename the file, and save the file in Photoshop format. To save a single-layer version for export, choose File > Save As and select the Save a Copy check box. Rename the file and save it in TIFF format or in a format supported by your presentation application.

Project 12: Create Photographic Backgrounds and Sidebars for Slide Presentations   85

Variation: Change the position of the sidebar template

Original template   **Flip Horizontal**

To create a number of different looks, try changing the orientation of a template. For example, by flipping the template, you can make the sidebar appear along the left or the right or along the top or the bottom of the slide. To change the orientation of a template, choose Image > Rotate > Flip Vertical or Flip Horizontal.

Variation: Add texture to the sidebar template

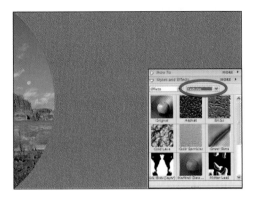

Apply a texture. After coloring the slide body in step 6 of the project, click the Styles and Effects arrow in the palette bin. Click the two separate pop-up menus and choose Filters and Textures. Now you will see only the filters that apply textures. If you are in List view, click the More pop-up menu and select Thumbnail View to see a preview of all of the textures.

Make sure that the Template layer is selected on the Layers palette and click a texture filter. To apply the filter, either click Apply or double-click the filter. If you want to try another filter, choose Edit > Undo (Ctrl/Cmd+Z) or press the Back arrow.

The right color for the body of your slide or the placement of a text shape can be critical. Start by looking at your presentation needs.

AVOID AWKWARD PLACEMENT
If you place your shape too low on a slide, it will be lopsided or cut off when it's projected.

BALANCE YOUR SHAPES
Try to center the shape in your image area. Choose View > Rulers for precise measurement guides.

CHOOSE YOUR COLORS WISELY
Make sure your colors will not make the text difficult to read.

MAKE YOUR TEXT THE FOCUS
Use neutral or subdued colors that promote the visibility of the slide contents.

Project 13

Create a PDF Slideshow

*Create an automated computer slideshow using the
PDF Slideshow feature of Photoshop Elements.*

The PDF Slideshow feature is terrific for creating a personal or professional slideshow for an online or desktop presentation. In this project you will also learn how to create a title slide from scratch and add it to your images. The steps have been broken apart for Mac and PC.

PC directions

1 **Organize your images.** Open the photo browser and make the necessary edits to the images you plan to use in the slideshow.

The slideshow will be shown full screen, so for the best image quality the size should be at least 1280 x 1024 pixels with a resolution of 72 pixels per inch. (See "Use the correct image size" on page 5.) After you are through editing the images, tag each of them or put them into a collection in the Organizer.

2

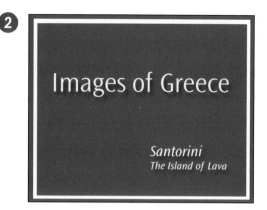

Create your title slide. In Photoshop Elements, choose File > New. For Height and Width, enter the same pixel values that you used for your slide images. The resolution should still be 72.

In the new file, select the color that you want to use for the background by clicking the Default Color icon (⬛). Select a color from the Color Picker that appears. Then click the Paint Bucket tool (⬧) and click anywhere in the image.

Finally, select the Type tool (T). Position the cursor in the center of the image. Click to enter your title text.

3 **Change the font and text color.** Double-click to select the text. On the options bar, use the pop-up menus to select different fonts and sizes. To change the color, simply click the color swatch on the options bar and use the Color Picker to select a new color.

Choose File > Save As and save the file in the Photoshop format in case you want to make changes later. Save it and place it with your other images in the Organizer. Note: To find out about creating a title slide with a photographic background, see Project 12.

4

Choose the slideshow images.

• In the Organizer or Editor click the Creations button.

• Choose Slide Show and click OK. Choose Simple PDF Slideshow and click OK. The Simple Slide Show dialog box will appear.

• Click on Add Photos.

• The Add Photos dialog box will appear. Select the Tag or Collection radio button depending on how you originally categorized your images. Use the pull-down menu to choose your set of images and click OK.

5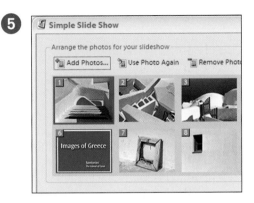

Set up your slideshow options. Now, back in the Simple Slide Show dialog box, drag and drop images into your preferred order. You can use Add Photo, Use Photo Again, and Remove Photo to edit your show.

6

Set up your final options. In the Slide Show Options area, you are going to set up your advanced timing, looping, and transitions.

The default setting for advancing the images is five seconds. If your slides are images only, this may be too long. If your slides have any text, this may be too short. Decide what time works best for your slides and enter that value. If you want the slideshow to repeat after it's finished, then select the Loop after Last Page check box.

Finally, choose the transition that you want to occur between slides. You may want to experiment to see which you like best.

7 **Save your slideshow.** At this point, you can save your file as Name.pdf or save it with a new name.

1 **Organize your images.** First make the necessary edits to the images you plan to use in the slideshow.

The slideshow will be shown full screen, so for the best image quality the size should be at least 1280 x 1024 pixels with a resolution of 72 pixels per inch. (For more information on sizing your images see "Use the correct image size" on page 5.) After you are through editing the images, place them all in one folder for easy access.

2

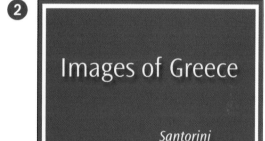

Create your title slide. In Photoshop Elements, choose File > New. For Height and Width, enter the same pixel values that you used for your slide images. The resolution should still be 72.

In the new file, select the color that you want to use for the background by clicking the Default Color icon (⬚). Select a color from the Color Picker that appears. Then click the Paint Bucket tool (⬤) and click anywhere in the image.

Finally, select the Type tool (T). Position the cursor in the center of the image. Click to enter your title text.

3 **Change the font and text color.** Double-click to select the text. On the options bar, use the pop-up menus to select different fonts and sizes. To change the color, simply click the color swatch on the options bar and use the Color Picker to select a new color.

Choose File > Save As and save the file in the Photoshop format in case you want to make changes later. Be sure to save it in the same folder as your other images.

Note: To find out about creating a title slide with a photographic background, see Project 12.

Choose the slideshow images. Choose File > Automation Tools > PDF Slideshow. Under Source Files, click Browse and navigate to the folder that contains your images. Select the folder and click Open.

When you are inside the folder, hold down the Shift key to select multiple images. After you have selected all of the images, click Open.

In the PDF Slideshow Source window, you will see a list of images. The slideshow will start with the image at the top of the list. You can reorder the images by clicking and dragging them into the correct sequence.

Output Options

Save as: ○ Multi-Page Document ● Slide Show
☐ View PDF after Saving

Slide Show Options
☑ Advance Every [5] Seconds
☐ Loop after Last Page
Transition: [Wipe Down ▾]

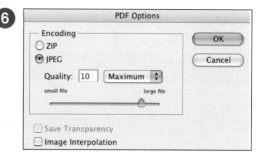

Set up your final options. Under Output Options select the Slide Show option.

In the Slide Show Options area, you are going to set up your advance timing, looping, and transitions.

The default setting for advancing the images is five seconds. If your slides are images only, this may be too long. If your slides have any text, this may be too short. Decide what time works best for your slides and enter that value. If you want the slideshow to repeat after it's finished, then select the Loop after Last Page check box.

Finally, choose the transition that you want to occur between slides. You may want to experiment to see which you like best.

Choose your compression. Click Advanced. This brings you to the PDF compression settings. The default setting is JPEG with a quality of Maximum. If you are posting this slideshow to the Web, you might want to make the Quality setting lower, to create a smaller file. The rest of the default settings are fine. Click OK to create your slideshow—and you're done.

Project 14

Create a Web Photo Gallery

Using nothing but your photographs and Photoshop Elements, you can create a sophisticated online gallery.

If you want to quickly post a gallery of images online, the Web Photo Gallery is just the thing. Photoshop Elements will create all of the HTML files as well as size and compress your images for the Web. The steps have been broken apart for Mac and PC.

Mac directions

Note: Photoshop Elements gives your HTML files the suffix .html or .htm. If you are uncertain which to use, choose .htm.

1 **Organize your image files.** First make the necessary edits to the images you will be posting to the Web.

Photoshop Elements will resize the images and compress a copy of them for the Web. To be sure you don't accidentally compress them twice, save the edited files in a PSD format. (For more information on compression formats, go to the online help in Photoshop Elements.)

After you have finished editing the images, place them in one folder for easy access. This will become your source folder.

Next, create a new folder. Give it a name that designates it as the destination for all the final files.

Select a gallery style. In Photoshop Elements, choose File > Create Web Photo Gallery. Your first task is to set the style of the gallery.

Click the pop-up Styles menu. When you select a style, a preview of it appears on the right side of the Web Gallery dialog box.

Some of the styles already have a finished look, while others are simple and allow for customizing. Select one that will work well with your images.

(Optional) In the Email text box, enter your e-mail address. The address will be a link in the title banner of the gallery.

3 **Set your source and destination.** Under Folders, click Choose. Navigate to the folder containing all of your images. Select the folder and click Open. Do the same for Destination, only this time choose the destination folder you created in step 1.

4

Create your title banner. Click the pop-up Options menu and select Banner. Enter the gallery title, the photographer's name, and the contact information.

5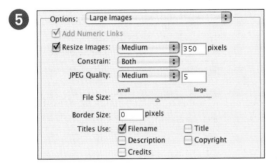

Set up your images. Click the Options pop-up menu again and choose Large Images. This dialog box is where you enter the size and compression you want to use when saving your Web images. Follow these steps for both the large images and image thumbnails:

• Make sure that the Resize Images check box is checked. On the pop-up menu next to it, you can choose Large (450 pixels), Medium (350 pixels), Small (250 pixels), or Custom. Select the size that you want. From the Constrain pop-up menu, specify whether you want your image size to be constrained horizontally or vertically.

• For JPEG Quality, select the setting that will work best with your images. Keep in mind that when you're saving JPEG images for the Web, medium or even low quality can be adequate. Higher-quality images that look great mean larger file sizes, and files that take longer to load on the screen.

• For Border Size, enter the pixel value you want for a border. If you don't want a border, enter 0.

• Select the check boxes for the text you want used as the image title. Titles, captions, and any copyright information will be taken from File Info, located on the File menu. Select the font and font size for the text.

6 **Set up security (optional).** The Security option is the last menu item on the Options pop-up menu.

The Security settings allow you to enter custom text, text for copyright information, titles, captions, and credits. To enter this information, select Security from the Options pop-up menu; then select an option from the Content pop-menu.

7 **You're done!** Click OK and your online gallery will be created and placed in your destination folder. At this point you can post it on the Web.

PC directions

1 **Organize your image files.** First make the necessary edits to the images you will be posting to the web. Photoshop Elements will resize the images and compress a copy of them for the Web. To be sure they are not accidentally compressed twice, save the files in a PSD format. After you are done editing the images add them to the Organizer if you have not already done so.

2

Select your gallery images. In the Organizer select the images you want to use for your photo gallery. At this point you can also tag them or create a new collection.

Place the images in the order that you want them to appear in the gallery.

With your images still selected click the Create button. Under Creation Setup click Web Photo Gallery and click OK. Under Adobe Web Photo gallery you will see your thumbnail images. If you'd like to add additional photos click the Add button.

Select your gallery style. Use the Gallery Style pop-up menu to select how you want your images to appear. You will see a preview of the layout underneath.

Create your title banner. Enter on information under the Banner tab.

Set your image sizes. Click on the Large Photos and Thumbnails tabs to set the sizes for your final gallery images.

Make sure that the Resize Photos check box is checked. On the pop-up menu next to it, you can choose Large, Medium, Small, or Custom. Select the size that you want, then set your image quality. Remember, the higher the quality, the larger the file and the slower the download.

Choose your destination. Click the Browse button in the Destination box. Navigate to where you want your Web gallery folder to be saved.

Click Save and you're done! At this point you can preview your gallery in any Web browser before posting it to the Web.

Variation: Change your colors

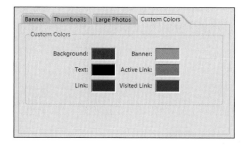

Customize the colors. If you used one of the basic frame or table styles for your gallery, you can easily customize the colors.

From the Options pop-up menu, select Custom Colors. Click the color swatches to change the colors of the text, links, background, and gallery banner.

Project 15

Create a Large, Mono-Color Background

Use a photo or illustration to make a large, mono-color background from brochures to Web pages.

If you have ever wanted to add an interesting background to the cover of a brochure or a Web page, this technique works great. Using a full-color image to fill an entire background would normally require a four-color process, which is costly, and for Web pages it would normally result in a file that's too large for Web viewing.

In this project, you create a mono-chromatic background that will result in lower printing costs and a smaller file size.

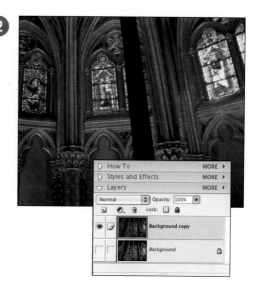

Get started. Open your color photo in Photoshop Elements and resize it as necessary. Note: Generally, for an image to fill the entire background of a Web page, it should be 600 to 800 pixels wide and at least 480 pixels high. The image size you choose should be based on the amount of material on the page.

For information on resizing images, (See "Use the correct image size" on page 5.)

Convert a copy of your background layer to black and white. If your Layers palette is not open, click the Layers arrow in the palette bin. Select your background layer and drag it over the Create a New Layer icon (⬜) located at the top of the Layers palette. With your new layer selected, choose Enhance > Adjust Color > Remove Color.

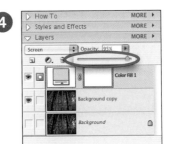

Adjust the color opacity. Select the new color layer on the Layers palette. Use the Opacity slider at the top of the palette to adjust the layer's opacity. This affects the intensity of the color and allows more of the grayscale image to show through.

Create a new color layer. You will use this color layer to colorize your black-and-white background. Choose Layer > New Fill Layer > Solid Color. In the New Layer dialog box, select Screen from the Mode pop-up menu and click OK. Then choose a color using the Color Picker that appears. Remember that this is your primary background color so select a color that will complement the rest of your artwork.

5 **Save a working version of the file.** Choose File > Save As and save the file in Photoshop format using a new name. This way, you will always have a version that contains all of your layers in case you want to make any changes.

Variation: Optimize the image for the Web

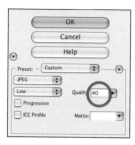

After you have saved the working version, choose File > Save for Web. In the Save for Web dialog box, you will see two images. One is the original, and one is a preview of the optimized version. When you select different optimization settings, the changes will be reflected in this preview window.

Select JPEG from the Settings pop-up menu in the upper-right corner of the dialog box. Use the Quality slider to adjust the amount the image is compressed. The higher the quality of the image, the larger the file size. Since you are posting this image on the Web, you need to keep the file size small. With this in mind, start with a quality setting of 15. Check the file size underneath the image preview.

Try to keep the file size to around 20K or less. When you are happy with the quality and file size, click OK to save the Web version.

Adding outside graphic elements to your background image that complement the other graphics in your layout can make your final image more dynamic.

KEEP IT CLEAR
Don't allow the elements in the background
to interfere with the page content.

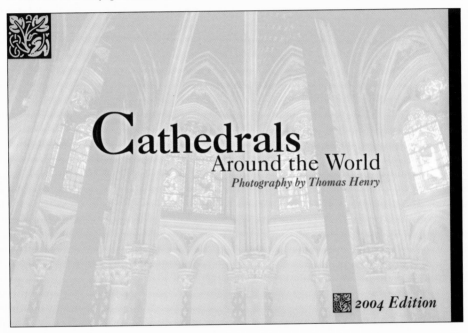

A color that is too dark or saturated decreases the legibility of text and can be distracting.

A soft or more neutral background color helps show off the rest of your content.

Project 16

Create Calendars, Cards, and Scrapbooks using Creations

Let Photoshop Elements' Creations automatically create a story with your images.

WINDOWS only

Have you ever wanted to create a card or a scrapbook as a gift or for a special occasion? The Creation feature in Photoshop Elements lets you do this quickly and easily using your digital images.

In this project you will learn how to create a scrapbook. The basic steps can also be used for other creations such as cards and calendars.

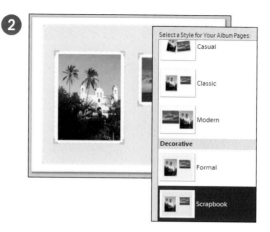

Get started. To begin, create a Collection with your images to start your project. In Organizer's Collections tabs click New and select images from the Photo Browser for your new collection. Save your new collection with the title for your scrapbook.

Note: If you need help with making a new collection see Project 17.

Choose your creation. Double-click your new collection icon so that you are viewing only those images. Next, click the Create icon (⊞). The images in your collection will automatically be selected for your scrapbook.

In Creation Setup dialog box choose Photo Album Pages and click OK. In Step 1 of the Create Photo Album Page dialog box choose the style of photo album and how many photos you want per page.

Step 2: Arrange Your Photos

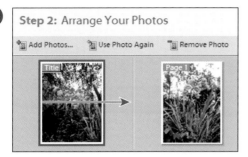

Arrange your photos. Once you can see all of your photos in the arrange window, simply click and drag them to where you want. They will automatically be resorted.

4

Add your captions. In the Customize dialog box, add the title of your scrapbook by double-clicking in the box below the title photo. Use the arrow keys on the side of the image to add the next caption. Click Next Step to save your creation.

Variation: Use the Editor to customize your scrapbook

Add some fun! Use the Photoshop Elements Editor to add borders, filters, or whatever you want to images destined for your scrapbook.

Project 17

Create Custom Photo Catalogs Using the Organizer

Using the Organizer in Photoshop Elements 3.0 for Windows you can create individual collections and categories of your entire image library.

WINDOWS only

While it looks like a simple photo display device, the Organizer is actually a powerful database that allows you to see images from various drives, folders, and email attachments all in one place.

In this project we will create a collection of photos similar to a traditional photo album. This is a really easy project that you will probably use often to organize your photos. In the second part of the project you will learn how to categorize your photos using tags. Both Collections and Tags are fantastic tools to keep track of all your images and allow you to find them in a snap.

Note: The photos you see in the Organizer are not actually stored there, but are still in their original folders. Be careful not to delete photos thinking that Organizer will save them. If you delete a photo from its original folder it will be gone and you won't be able to recover it.

Create a Collection in the Organizer

 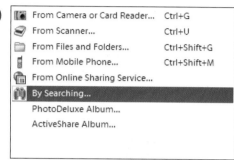

Get started. If you have not already brought your photos into Photoshop Elements 3 now is the time. Go to Organizer, open File and choose Get Photos > By Searching. Photoshop Elements will find all the photo files in your computer and open them in the Photo Browser. If you want, you can also bring in images from a variety of other sources.

Add your photos. Repeat the process for all the photos you want to put in your collection. To make it easier, Shift-select the photos into a single group and drag them to your new collection.

Double-click the icon in the Collections pane to view your new collection. That's it!

When you are done click Back to All Photos to view all of your photos.

Create a new collection. With all your images now in view you can find those you want to put in your first collection. Select the Collections tab in the right pane. Click New > New Collection. In the Create Collection dialog box type the subject name and any notes. Click OK.

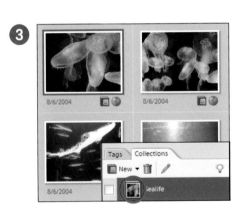

Create the icon. First, choose a bold, up-close photo so it will be recognizable as the Collection thumbnail. From the Collection pane either drag the photo onto the gray icon or drag the gray icon onto the photo. That photo will now appear as your Collection thumbnail.

Create Tags in the Organizer

Tags let you mark photos and put them into categories and subcategories. Inside the Tags pane there are also preexisting categories of people, places, and things where you can store your finished tags. For example, say you collect animal photos, lots of them. With tags you can tag all of your animal photos "Animals" and make subcategories such as "Zoo," "Farm," "Forest," "Birds," and "Aquarium." The possibilities are endless.

In this project you will tag a set of photos and then create a subcategory.

1

Create a new tag. In the Organizer click on the Tags tab and click New > New Tag. Here fill in the name of the subject and any notes you have. You will now see the new gray icon in the Create Tag pane. Drag the icon to the photo you choose to represent the tag or vice versa, as you did with your collections.

2 **Add your photos.** Repeat dragging the icon into every photo in this category. If you want to simplify this process you can Shift-select a group of photos and drag the icon to the group, as you did with your collections.

3

Create a subcategory. First select the category you want to add to. In the Tags tab select New > New Sub-category. In the dialog box input the name and click OK. Drag the new icon onto the photos you want to include in your new category. You can keep adding subcategories.

4 **Get organized!** To further organize your photos you can sort your tags into the icons for favorites, people, friends, places, and events. If you have photos you do not want displayed, you can tag them with the hidden icon.

Index

Production Notes

This book was created electronically using
Adobe Indesign CS. Art was produced using
Adobe Illustrator CS, Adobe Photoshop CS, and
Adobe Photoshop Elements 3.0.

Photography Credits

Lisa Matthews

All photographs with the exception of Projects
4 and Project 11.

Julianne Kost

Project 4 (all photos)

Elizabeth Pham

Project 11 (introductory wedding photo)